THE BIOGRAPHY

BILLY CONNOLLY BOOK

By Paul Christey

Copyright © 2023 [Paul Christey] All rights reserved. No part of this publication may be reproduced, distributed, or transmitted in any form or by any means, including photocopying, recording, or other electronic or mechanical methods, without the prior written permission of the publisher.

Table of Contents

Foreword..4
Introduction 7
Chapter 1 14
   Billy Connolly: Who He Is...........................14

Chapter 2 24

   The Making of a Musician 24

Chapter 3 32

   The Humblebum Band's Departure and Billy's Transformation into a Comedian 32

Chapter 4 42

   Connolly's Ascendance to Fame in the UK 42

Chapter 5 48

   Billy Connolly: A Life Beyond the Stage 48

Chapter 6 56

   Billy Connolly's Achievement Awards: The Legendary Comedian 56

Foreword

There aren't many names in comedy that are as well-known as Billy Connolly. His distinct sense of humor and inspiring life narrative have enthralled audiences all around the world for decades. You will travel through this iconic entertainer's amazing life in the pages that follow.

A personal and incisive image of a man whose humor has won the hearts of millions is presented in the biography of Billy Connolly. Connolly's life narrative is one of tenacity, originality, and unrestrained wit, starting with his early years spent on the streets of Glasgow and ending with his ascent to international prominence.

This biography goes deep into Connolly's life, exposing the struggles and victories that helped him become the well-liked person we know today. Every aspect of Connolly's life is carefully and precisely examined, from his modest beginnings to his breakthrough comedic career, from his inner battles to his unwavering spirit. You will learn more about the comic with a heart as large as his humor as you read through the pages of this book. You'll learn about the difficulties he overcame, the friendships he made, and the influence he had on comedy and other fields.

The voyage of Billy Connolly will move you, amuse you, and occasionally make you cry. This biography promises to be an engaging and instructive experience, regardless of whether you have been a fan for a long time or are only now learning about his work. Allow yourself to be swept away into the world of Billy Connolly as you turn the next few pages to experience his sense of humor, kindness, and unrelenting zest for life. As Billy himself would say, "Never trust a man who, when left alone in a room with a tea cozy, doesn't try it on." Have fun on the voyage and keep in mind this advice.

Introduction

Billy Connolly is one of the few names in the world of comedy that stands out from the crowd. Billy Connolly is regarded as an icon in the entertainment industry. His life and work have had a profound impact on comedy, music, and the hearts of innumerable people all over the world. We delve deeply into the life and times of a man whose wit, charm, and irreverence have made him a revered figure for generations as we set off on this voyage through the pages of "Billy Connolly: The Biography," which is a biography of the actor.

Billy Connolly's journey from Glasgow, Scotland, to the top of the comedy world is a monument to the strength of humor, tenacity, and following one's passions. Connolly, who was born on November 24, 1942, in a working-class neighborhood, encountered early difficulties that influenced his distinct viewpoint and comic approach. He discovered that using humor to get through tough times and connect with others while growing up in post-war Britain.

This biography of Billy Connolly takes the reader on a trip through his various stages of life rather than just detailing his professional life. We go into his formative infancy, when the seeds of his comedic brilliance were planted, and we follow him through the turbulent adolescent. Connolly first became enamored with music during these formative years; this affinity would go on to remarkably entwine with his comedy.

Connolly's transformation from a shipyard worker to a folk musician as he enters his teenage years is something we see as we learn more about his upbringing in the 1960s and his involvement in bands. Along with enhancing his musical abilities, his experiences in the folk movement exposed him to a variety of oddball people and stories that subsequently found a home in his stand-up comedy performances.

Connolly didn't truly embrace the world of stand-up comedy until the early 1970s. His on-stage debut took place at Glasgow's illustrious Halfway to Paradise Club, ushering in a famous career. He had a compelling stage presence, great storytelling skills, and a razor-sharp humor that captured audiences right away. Connolly had definitely discovered his true calling.

We examine Connolly's ground-breaking comedy specials throughout the biography, from "Billy Connolly: An Audience with..." through "Billy and Albert." He had an unmatched talent to turn the mundane into hilarious treasure. He approached everything with a sense of humor that was both perceptive and hilarious, from commonplace observations to the complexity of human nature. He became popular with audiences all around the world because of his ability to discover humor in everyday situations.

Connolly's venture into acting gave his brilliant career another facet in addition to his comedic work. His roles in movies like "Mrs. Brown" and "The Man Who Sued God" demonstrated his range as a performer and won him praise from critics. His slick switch between comedy and drama cemented his reputation as a genuine entertainer.

Connolly's personal life has served as a source of inspiration and reflection in addition to his professional accomplishments. His candor in discussing his struggles with addiction and his 2013 Parkinson's disease diagnosis helped to bring to light the difficulties he encountered with unshakable honesty and humor. His fortitude in the face of adversity serves as a reminder that even the funniest people suffer from time to time.

It's impossible to ignore Billy Connolly's influence on the comedy industry as we consider his remarkable journey. He cleared the path for future generations of comedians by dismantling constraints and expanding the definition of comedy. Numerous comedians who came after him still use humorous techniques that show his impact.

In "Billy Connolly: The Biography," we make an effort to convey the core of this exceptional man—the comedian, musician, actor, and person. We seek to present a thorough and intimate portrayal of a guy whose laughter has been a continuous companion for millions through in-depth research and interviews with people who have come into contact with Connolly.

Prepare to be entertained, informed, and inspired as you go through Billy Connolly's life, dear reader, as you begin this voyage. Billy Connolly's life narrative is one of victory, humor, and the enduring power of laughter, from the laughter-filled stages of comedy clubs to the quiet moments of reflection. Welcome to the "Billy Connolly" universe.

Chapter 1

Billy Connolly: Who He Is

The renowned Scottish comedian and actor, Billy Connolly, is adored in the entertainment industry. His fascinating life, which was full of humor and wit, has left a lasting impression on the hearts of millions of people.

In Anderston, Glasgow, Scotland, on November 24, 1942, Billy Connolly was born. His early life was marked by hardship and poverty because he was raised in a working-class family. Engineers were a common profession in Glasgow at the time, and William Connolly Sr.'s father was one among them. At the dock, the Connolly family resided. Connolly typically drew humor from his experiences growing up in a household where funds were frequently tight, therefore his blue-collar background would later become a recurrent motif in his comedy. His mother, Mary McLean Connolly, was a cafeteria worker at the hospital. Billy Connolly's personality and sense of humor were significantly influenced by his family upbringing. Billy has elder siblings named Florence and Michael in the Connolly family.

Connolly experienced the hardships and difficulties that many families in post-war Scotland suffered as a result of growing up in a working-class setting. The Connolly family is primarily Catholic and has some Irish ancestry.

He was born in a turbulent time and was known to everyone as Billy. Glasgow, like many other cities, was ravaged by the Second World War. Because of his parents' modest upbringing—William Connolly Sr. and Mary McLean—young Billy was raised in accordance with the working-class values of the time. Childhood for Billy Connolly was filled with both happiness and hardship. He was hospitalized for several months after contracting the crippling disease polio when he was four years old. Connolly's attitude on life was significantly affected by this early experience with illness and vulnerability. He frequently highlighted how the encouragement and humor of his hospital colleagues and fellow patients helped him deal with the difficulties of his sickness.

Connolly made a remarkable recovery and restored his mobility despite the polio-related difficulties. His humorous approach was defined by his tenacity and capacity to find humor in even the most trying circumstances. Connolly frequently made jokes about having polio, turning a traumatic memory into a source of amusement for viewers all around the world.

Billy experienced several difficulties throughout his formative years, including living in a small tenement. He stopped attending school when he was 15 and worked a variety of occupations, such as delivery boy and shipyard welder. Despite these early setbacks, Connolly's wit and humor started to mature around this time, and he started playing in neighborhood bands and folk music ensembles, laying the groundwork for his later comedic career.

Connolly grew up in poverty. Before deciding to pursue a career in entertainment, he held a number of professions, including that of a welder in a shipyard. He first played with Gerry Rafferty in a band named The Humblebums in the late 1960s before becoming well-known as a folk singer and pianist.

Billy had a challenging beginning to his life. His mother abandoned him when he was only four years old. This heartbreaking blow had a long-lasting effect on his life and sense of humor. Billy was raised by his father and his aunts Margaret and Mona Connolly, and his early years were anything but typical. Although he went to St. Peter's Primary School and St. Gerard's Secondary School, he never achieved academic achievement.

Connolly began a series of odd occupations as a teenager. He supported his love of music by working as a delivery boy, an apprentice welder in a shipyard, and even as a boilermaker. His early experiences in these challenging, blue-collar settings eventually served him an abundant supply of fodder for his stand-up comedy.

In his formative years, Billy's relationship with music was quite important. He started playing the guitar and banjo and became passionate about folk music. He finally joined the folk band "The Humblebums" with future actor and comedian Gerry Rafferty thanks to his musical abilities. Connolly started experimenting with humor on stage during this time, despite the band's modest success.

Billy Connolly had a complicated formal education. He went to St. Peter's School in Glasgow's Partick neighborhood, but he subsequently acknowledged that he wasn't a responsible student. Following in the footsteps of his father, he pursued a career as a welder in the Glasgow shipyards thanks to his early passion in painting and the arts. Connolly's experience as a welder gave him plenty of fodder for his comedic work. He frequently recalled amusing tales from his time working in the shipyards, providing a window into the working-class culture and camaraderie that characterized that setting.

His capacity for finding humor in the banal and commonplace won him the hearts of audiences who could identify with his circumstances.

Connolly never lost interest in the arts, though. He pursued his passion for folk music in his free time and started playing in neighborhood bands. He later became interested in stand-up comedy as a result of this. Although his early attempts at comedy met with varying degrees of success, he persisted and continued to hone his craft and develop his distinctive style.

Billy started his apprenticeship at the age of 16 and completed it at the age of 21. He stayed there until he became 22. Billy then decided to pursue a welding apprenticeship, which he completed when he was 24. There were six ships being constructed when he first started as an apprentice. He gained a lot from the experience, learning how males interact with one another. Alongside other craftsmen like welders, caulkers, players, engineers, electricians, burners, and joiners, he worked on various projects. Billy will never forget Bobby Dalgleish and Jimmy Lucas, who were instrumental in helping him hone his comedic and welding abilities.

The impact Billy Connolly has had on comedy is tremendous. Through his humor, he not only delighted millions of people but also disregarded conventions and questioned them.

Chapter 2
The Making of a Musician

His early years were difficult because he was raised in a working-class family in one of Glasgow's worst areas. During his formative years, Connolly found comfort in music. He picked up the guitar and the banjo and developed a love of folk music that would last his entire life.

Connolly began his musical career by playing in Glasgow's busy downtown streets as a street musician. He performed folk songs and told tales through his music, frequently finding inspiration in the day-to-day activities of those around him. His early exposure to Glasgow's thriving folk music scene had a profound impact on his artistic sensibility.

The folk music renaissance swept the United States and the United Kingdom in the 1960s. Young listeners' hearts and minds were being captured by artists like Woody Guthrie, Joan Baez, and Bob Dylan through their moving folk music. Billy Connolly, who was captivated to the folk music's raw emotion and narrative ability, was also impacted by this trend.

Connolly spent time on the City's Rose Street, where he frequented various pubs, while attending the Edinburgh Festival Fringe for the first time in the early 1960s. He became friends with some well-known long-haired musicians and chose to adopt their look. In 1965, Billy finished his five-year boilermaker apprenticeship. He spent ten weeks working for a short time in a Nigerian oil company. After arriving in the UK, he worked for John Brown & Company until leaving to concentrate on his musical career, specifically folk music.

After watching "The Beverly Hillbillies," he went out and bought his first banjo at the Barrowland monument. He then embarked on a music tour and made frequent appearances at the Scotia pub on Stockwell Street with well-known folk singer Danny Kyle. The two performed together on multiple occasions after being introduced to folk clubs including Saturday Late and Montrose Street Gasglow Folk Club, among others. Connolly's musical career improved in 1969 after he and Tam Harvey created a folk-pop group. Gerry Rafferty, who had met Billy after a Paisley performance, later joined the group. The group's name was "Humblebums". They signed with the "Transatlantic Records" independent record company and went on to release one album. While Billy and Rafferty put out two more albums, The Humblebums in 1969 and Open up the Door in 1970, Harvey departed the group.

Since it was the start of his comedic career, Rafferty's time with Billy turned into an interesting season in his career. While waiting to take the stage, Rafferty made joking phone calls; these antics used to make Billy shout with laughter. He hasn't yet made a full transition towards comedy, though.

At the age of 26, Connolly married Irish Pressagh, a professional interior designer and native of Ireland, and became a family man.

The couple got divorced after having two kids together. After 22 years, Billy Connolly and his mother, who worked in the cafeteria of a local general hospital, met again at a Humblebum concert in Dunoon. Since she abandoned Connolly, they had met up once more. With her new companion Willie Adams, for whom she gave birth to three daughters and a son, Mary had been residing in the town. After the Humblebums performance, Billy decided to spend the night at her mother's house rather than a hotel. The "Welly Boot Song" is one of Connolly's best-known musical compositions from this time period. Connolly's ability to flawlessly combine music and comedy is on full display in this song with its catchy tune and witty lyrics. It became a mainstay of his live performances and a fan favorite.

Connolly's album "Cop Yer Whack For This" is among his most illustrious musical accomplishments from this era. The CD, which was released in 1974, mixed stand-up comedy with original music. It showed Connolly's determination to push the bounds of entertainment and distinguished it from the conventional comedy albums of the time.

Billy Connolly's opportunity to pursue his musical passions on a broader platform increased along with his notoriety. He performed on stages all around the world, delighting audiences with his distinct humor and musical style. During musical interludes during his live concerts, he would frequently take up his banjo and enchant the crowd with sentimental tunes and humorous stories.

Connolly's participation in the 1984 charity event "The Secret Policeman's Ball" was one of the turning points in his musical career. Many well-known comedians and artists performed at this Amnesty International event. The show's high point was Connolly's performance, which combined comedy and song while also promoting human rights problems.

Billy Connolly's music evolved over the years from a career ambition to more of a personal escape. In his free time, he continued to play the banjo and guitar, finding comfort and delight in the melodies he composed. Even though his health was having serious problems, music remained his constant friend.

Chapter 3

The Humblebum Band's Departure and Billy's Transformation into a Comedian

In 1971, the Humblebums broke up, with Rafferty going on to record his solo album

"Can I have my money back" and Connolly resuming his career in folk music. He continued to advance his comedic career with Nat Joseph's assistance. Connolly had the ability to be funny, and Joseph could see that. He had previously assisted the well-known Scottish entertainer Hamish Imlach in developing his music recording career. Recognizing Connolly's talent, he counseled him to abandon folk music and concentrate on comedy.

Billy Connolly is renowned for his distinct brand of comedy and his storytelling prowess. Billy Connolly made a gradual but significant move from musician to comedian. He realized his innate talent for humor and storytelling while performing with "The Humblebums." The best parts of their performances eventually were his anecdotes and banter with the audience. Connolly made the decision to pursue solo comedy when the band's success began to decline. Connolly, known as the Big Yin of comedy, is a household figure among fans of humor everywhere. Connolly has made an imprint on the comedy industry that will never be erased during the course of a multi-decade career.

In his teenage years, Connolly used the moniker "The Big Yin" to set himself apart from his enormous and powerful father. Billy eventually outgrew his father in size. One of his followers referred to him as "The Big Yin" during one of his performances at the bar.

Connolly's musical career gave him a stage on which to display his engaging on-stage persona and clever banter in between songs. Audiences started to discover his inherent comic talent about this time. He frequently used observational humour, bizarre anecdotes, and the usage of his distinctive Scottish accent in his humor. For Connolly, the switch from comedy to music was not something he had anticipated. It developed naturally as a result of how well-received his hilarious interludes during music concerts were by audiences. He started adding more humor to his performances and gradually shifted his attention away from stand-up comedy and toward music.

His performance on the British television program "Parkinson" in the early 1970s served as a turning point in his comic career. This performance signaled a turning point in his life, captivating the crowd with his humorous and lively narration. He began to be more widely known as a comic than a musician.

When Connolly began doing stand-up comedy in the early 1970s, his humorous career really took off. Even though his early appearances were in modest bars and clubs, his talent quickly became well known. He immediately won over audiences with his observant comedy, loud Scottish accent, and wild hair. Connolly's debut comedy CD, "Billy Connolly Live!" was well-received by critics when it was published in 1975. This was the first of a string of lucrative comedy albums and live shows that propelled him to celebrity in the UK and elsewhere.

Connolly's fame quickly grew outside of the UK. He was introduced to worldwide audiences on his first global tour in the late 1970s, especially in North America, where his humour was well received. He became a well-liked character in the comedy world thanks to his capacity to relate to people from all walks of life. Connolly's stand-up comedy albums and specials are some of his most important creations. His critically lauded records include "Billy Connolly: Live at the Odeon Hammersmith" and "Billy Connolly: The Pick of Billy Connolly". He further cemented his reputation as a comedic classic by appearing in various TV shows and films.

As a result of his developing fame, he became friends with other famous people, including important figures in the music business like Elton John, who wanted to help his favorite British artists succeed in the United States. During his 1976 US tour, John attempted to promote Connolly's popularity in the country by utilizing him as the opening act. However, the strategy failed because John's American fans showed no interest in the comedian.

The 1985 television program "An Audience with Billy Connolly" featured Connolly's comic brilliance in front of a live audience. Viewers were intrigued by his humorous antics, razor-sharp wit, and distinctive storytelling approach. One of his most cherished performances is still "An Audience with Billy Connolly."

"Billy Connolly: Live at the Odeon Hammersmith London" (1991): Connolly's ability to riff on commonplace observations and his contagious enthusiasm were on full display in this presentation. He spoke on a variety of subjects, including family life and Scottish culture, and his ability to engage the audience was clear throughout the event.

Although he is best known for his stand-up, Connolly also dabbled in acting in "The Man Who Sued God" (2001). He portrayed Steve Myers, the main character in the comedy "The Man Who Sued God," who accuses the church of being the victim of an act of God. Connolly's strong presence and humorous timing were evident, and the movie stands out as a noteworthy addition to his discography.

"Billy Connolly: Erect for 30 Years" (2003): Connolly celebrated his 30th year in the entertainment business with this spectacular. It was a celebration of his professional accomplishments and evidence of his ongoing appeal. He jokingly pondered on his life, his celebrity, and the changes he had seen over the years in this program.

Connolly kept performing and touring into his older years, as seen by his 2016 "High Horse Tour" album. His tenacity and continuing comedic talent were demonstrated by the "High Horse Tour". Connolly amused audiences with his typical comedy and storytelling despite struggling with his health.

Connolly's appeal cut beyond national boundaries, and his comedic style connected with individuals from all backgrounds. In addition to being a comedian, he was also a storyteller, philosopher, and social critic. Connolly's place as a national treasure in Scotland and a renowned figure in the entertainment business was cemented in 2017 when he was knighted for his contributions to entertainment and philanthropy.

The career of Billy Connolly opened doors for several comedians and entertainers. His capacity to engage audiences via humor and storytelling created a lasting impression on the comedy community. His impact can be observed in the comedy of others who came after him.

Chapter 4

Connolly's Ascendance to Fame in the UK

Billy was talented off the stage as well. He transitioned to television with ease and became well-known in the UK. His appearances on programs such as "The Billy Connolly Show" and "Billy Connolly's World Tour of Scotland" furthered his reputation as a comic legend. In addition, he dabbled in acting, landing prominent parts in movies including "Mrs. Brown" and "The Boondock Saints." The entertainment business will never be the same because of Billy Connolly's work on television and in cinemas.

The 1970s saw Connolly's big break on television when he made appearances on British TV programs including "Parkinson" and "The Wheeltappers and Shunters Social

Club." These early roles demonstrated his comedic talent and set the stage for a prosperous television career.

"The Billy Connolly Show," which debuted in the late 1970s, was one of Connolly's most well-known television projects. His stand-up humor, skits, and musical performances were featured on this program. It not only confirmed his position as the best comedian in the UK but also made him known to a wider audience. Billy Connolly made his Hollywood debut in the 1980s and starred in movies including "Water" and "The Return of the Musketeers." He left a lasting impression on the big screen because to his amiable demeanor and distinctive sense of humor. His popularity in the UK remained strong because to programs like "An Audience with Billy Connolly."

Live performances in theaters by Billy Connolly were very important to his career. He rose to fame as a result of his funny and upbeat stand-up performances. He performed at a number of notable locations, including the London's Hammersmith Apollo. Live performances by Connolly frequently sold out.

Martin Lewis, a renowned producer, extended an invitation to Connolly in 1979 to join the cast of "The Secret Policeman's Ball," a production that raised money for Amnesty

International. Connolly made history as the first comedian to perform in the series, and he made multiple appearances in the film. He had the chance to create friendly ties with well-known actors like John Cleese and Peter Cook as a result of the development.

He received another invitation from Martin Lewis and John Cleese in 1981 to take part in that year's "The secret policeman's other Bail" episode. His reputation with Americans increased as a result of the film's success as they got to know his comic fans, which prompted him to come back eight years later. Billy Connolly debuted in North America in the 1970s and went on to feature in a number of American films, but he didn't become well-known until 1990, when he made a cameo in the HBO special Whoopi Goldberg, which was created by the Brooklyn Academy of Music in New York. Additionally, he participated in "The War Song of the Urpneys" alongside renowned boxers Ozzy Osbourne and Frank Burno.

Connolly held a concert in June 1992 to commemorate his 25th birthday. Billy was well accepted because the entire event was covered by the BBC. He came to Australia in 1995 after finishing a 40-day globe tour that began with a 40-day stop in Scotland.

Connolly was devastated when he lost Danny Kyle, his best friend, to the icy grip of death in 1998. Prior to that, he had lost both his mother Mary McLean and father William Connolly, who both died of strokes in March 1988. After a fight with motor neurone illness for five years.

Chapter 5

Billy Connolly: A Life Beyond the Stage

In addition to being a comedy legend, Billy Connolly is a powerful advocate for charity. His generous endeavors and philanthropic deeds have had a profound effect on many charitable initiatives. Connolly has long been a cherished name in the entertainment world. Connolly has been involved in several charitable endeavors and altruistic acts that have affected the lives of many people, in addition to his humorous abilities. Connolly has supported numerous philanthropic groups and causes throughout the years, using his notoriety and power to improve society.

While Billy Connolly's humor made many people smile and laugh, he also understood the value of giving back to the community and championing issues that were important to him. His philanthropic endeavors are evidence of his compassion and drive to improve society. Connolly participated in Comic Relief, a UK-based organization that utilizes humor to generate money for a variety of causes, such as healthcare and poverty alleviation programs. This was one of Connolly's significant charitable endeavors.

He actively participated in initiatives to enhance the lives of kids, people with disabilities, and cancer patients. His participation in fundraising events including benefit concerts, auctions, and walks demonstrated how committed he was to making a difference. Connolly was incredibly frank about his own health issues, which was one of the most admirable features of his charitable deeds. He disclosed in 2013 that he had received diagnoses for prostate cancer and Parkinson's disease the same day. He bravely made the decision to use his platform to spread awareness about these issues rather than slink away from the spotlight.

Billy Connolly's devotion to the humanities has also manifested itself in his charitable endeavors. He has backed programs that advance the arts, such as giving young artists scholarships and supporting cultural organizations. Connolly's commitment to the welfare of children is yet another important facet of his charitable endeavors. He has helped groups like Children in Need, which works to better the lives of underprivileged children in the UK, through the Big Yin Charitable Trust. His contributions have made it possible for kids suffering hardship to have access to essential resources and opportunities.

The Big Yin Charitable Trust was established in 2001 by Pamela Stephenson, the spouse of Billy Connolly. Connolly's charitable endeavors have been focused on this nonprofit foundation. The trust is committed to helping a number of causes, such as the arts, children's welfare, and healthcare. It has made considerable financial contributions to several nonprofit organizations, significantly improving the lives of individuals who are less fortunate.

He supports The Celtic and the National Association for Bikers with Disabilities.

Connolly has written comic books in the past. From 1973 to 1977, he co-wrote "The Big Yin," a newspaper daily comic with cartoonist Malky McCormick. He also enjoys the arts. Over eleven volumes of Connolly's artwork have been released. In Kirkcudbright, Scotland, MacLellan's Castle was projected with one of his works of art as part of the 2019 World Parkinson Day celebrations. His first piece of art was motivated by his prior experience as a welder.

While Billy Connolly's career was flourishing, his personal life also had ups and downs. He has two children with his first wife, Iris Pressagh, whom he married in 1969. Their marriage ended in divorce in 1985, and he was given custody of Jamie and Cara.

He wed Pamela Stephenson, a fellow comedian and psychologist, in 1989; they have three kids together. After the comedian from New Zealand made an appearance at the BBC sketch show, where she was one of the four regular performers, the two became friends in 1979. For the second time on his 84-day Big Wee Tour of Britain, Connollyet Stephenson. The two met in Brighton's backstage area. They kept their friendship going and later began dating.

Parkinson's Disease: A Difficult Time for Billy Connolly

Billy Connolly has experienced serious health issues recently. He revealed that he has Parkinson's disease, a degenerative neurological ailment, in 2013. He persevered in the face of this diagnosis and carried on performing, sharing his experience with audiences and bringing attention to the illness.

Even for someone whose humor had made countless people laugh, Billy Connolly's health issues served as a sobering reminder of the frailty of life. Connolly definitely suffered from the initial shock and uncertainty of his diagnosis, as everyone who experiences such a serious health setback does.

Chapter 6
Billy Connolly's Achievement Awards: The Legendary Comedian

The Big Yin, also known as Billy Connolly, is a legendary personality in the entertainment industry, renowned for his unmatched talent in music, comedy, and theater. Connolly has made an enduring impact on the industry throughout the course of a career spanning more than five decades, garnering countless awards and accolades in the process. In this thorough investigation, we will delve into his incredible career and showcase his accomplishments, notoriety, and influence in these three separate but related areas of the entertainment industry.

Billy Connolly has over the years produced a number of comedic albums and DVDs, all of which feature his distinct humor. Among his most well-known productions are "Billy Connolly: Live at the Odeon Hammersmith London," "The Man Who Sued God," and "Billy Connolly's World Tour of Scotland." His hilarious brilliance was preserved for future generations by these recordings, which perfectly caught the essence of his live performances.

Billy Connolly excelled in humor and music, and he also made substantial contributions to the theater. As the lead in the Tony Award-winning show "Billy Connolly: Live at the Royal Opera House" in 1991, he played one of his most illustrious theatrical roles. He received praise from critics for his great performance in this theatrical production and his storytelling prowess.

Connolly created a name for himself on the big screen as well, acting in a number of movies like "Mrs. Brown" (1997), for which he was nominated for a BAFTA Award. His agility and breadth as an actor allowed him to effortlessly switch between comedy, drama, and even fantastical genres.

Billy Connolly has had a significant impact on the entertainment industry with his amazing talent. He has won numerous honors and distinctions over his career, which attest to his influence on the sector. His most prominent accolades include:

For his extraordinary achievements to film and television, Connolly was honored with multiple BAFTA Awards, including the 2003 BAFTA Scotland Lifetime Achievement Award.

Tony Awards: In 1991, his portrayal of Billy Connolly in "Billy Connolly: Live at the Royal Opera House" won him a Tony Award for Best Special Theatrical Event.

National Television Awards: For his outstanding work in humor, Connolly received numerous National Television Awards from the British public.

He won several comedy prizes, solidifying his position as an icon of the genre.

Awards from the British Academy Scotland recognized Connolly's impact in Scotland, including the Outstanding Contribution to Television Award in 2016.

The influence of Billy Connolly on the entertainment business is enormous. His seamless transitions between comedy, theatre, and music not only showed his flexibility, but also his true enthusiasm for delighting crowds. Connolly paved the path for a new generation of comedians with his boldness in tackling taboo subjects and his storytelling skills.

Beyond his professional accomplishments, Connolly has touched many people's hearts with his candor about his struggle with Parkinson's disease and his support of awareness and research. His fortitude in the face of hardship has inspired and touched people all across the world.

Printed in Great Britain
by Amazon